God Bless America

Words and music by Irving Berlin

Illustrations by Lynn Munsinger

HarperCollins*Publishers*

God bless America,

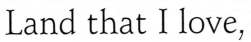

Land that I love,

Stand beside her

And guide her

Through the night with a light from above.

From the mountains,

To the prairies,

To the oceans white with foam,

God bless America,

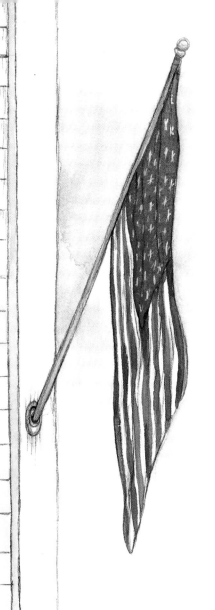

My home sweet home.

God Bless America

Words and Music by
IRVING BERLIN

While the storm clouds gather * Far across the sea,
Let us swear allegiance * To a land that's free;
Let us all be grateful * For a land so fair,
As we raise our voices * In a solemn prayer.

God bless A - mer - i - ca,_____ land
that I love._____ Stand be - side her_____ and
guide her_____ thru the night with a light from a - bove._____

"God Bless America" by Irving Berlin was first published in 1938. Almost as soon as the song began generating revenue, Mr. Berlin established the God Bless America Fund to benefit American youth. Most of the earnings from "God Bless America" have been donated to two youth organizations with which Mr. and Mrs. Berlin were personally involved: the Girl Scout Council of Greater New York, and the Greater New York Councils of the Boy Scouts of America. These councils do not discriminate on any basis and are committed to serving all segments of New York City's diverse youth population.

The trustees of the God Bless America Fund are working with the two councils to ensure that funding is allocated for New York City children affected by the tragic events of September 11, 2001.

A portion of the publisher's proceeds is also being donated to the God Bless America Fund.

To the children of New York and
their friends everywhere

—L.M.

God Bless America • © Copyright 1938, 1939 by Irving Berlin • © Copyright Renewed 1965, 1966 by Irving Berlin • © Copyright Assigned to the Trustees of the God Bless America Fund • International Copyright Secured • All Rights Reserved. Used by Permission. • Illustrations copyright © 2002 by Lynn Munsinger • Printed in the U.S.A. • www.harperchildrens.com • Library of Congress Cataloging-in-Publication Data • Berlin, Irving, (date). • God Bless America / lyrics by Irving Berlin ; illustrations by Lynn Munsinger. • p.   cm. • Summary: A family of bears experiences America in an illustrated version of the classic song. • ISBN 0-06-009788-4 — ISBN 0-06-009789-2 (lib. bdg.) • 1. Children's songs—United States—Texts. • 2. United States—Songs and music. • [1. United States—Songs and music. 2. Songs.] • I. Munsinger, Lynn, ill. • II. Title. • PZ8.3.B4565 Go 2002 • 2002002154 • 782.421599'0268—dc21 • CIP AC • Typography by Jeanne L. Hogle
1 2 3 4 5 6 7 8 9 10 ❖ First Edition